Based on the best-selling piano method by Kenneth Baker.

THE COMPLETE PIANO PLAYER
LES MISÉRABLES

Wise Publications
London/New York/Paris/Sydney/Copenhagen/Berlin/Madrid/Hong Kong/Tokyo

Exclusive distributors:
Music Sales Limited
14-15 Berners Street,
London W1T 3LJ, UK.
Music Sales Pty Limited
Units 3-4, 17 Willfox Street, Condell Park
NSW 2200, Australia.

This book © Copyright 2014 by Wise Publications.
Order No. AM1008337
ISBN: 978-1-78305-449-7

Arranged by Derek Jones.
Processed by Paul Ewers Music Design.
Edited by Ruth Power.

Printed in the EU.

Your Guarantee of Quality
As publishers, we strive to produce every book to the
highest commercial standards.
This book has been carefully designed to minimise awkward page turns
and to make playing from it a real pleasure.
Particular care has been given to specifying acid-free, neutral-sized
paper made from pulps which have not been elemental chlorine bleached.
This pulp is from farmed sustainable forests and was produced with
special regard for the environment.
Throughout, the printing and binding have been planned to ensure a sturdy,
attractive publication which should give years of enjoyment.
If your copy fails to meet our high standards, please
inform us and we will gladly replace it.

www.musicsales.com

A Little Fall Of Rain

Music by Claude-Michel Schönberg
Original Lyrics by Alain Boublil & Jean-Marc Natel
English Lyrics by Herbert Kretzmer

So don't you fret M'sieur Mar - ius, I don't feel an - y pain._____ A

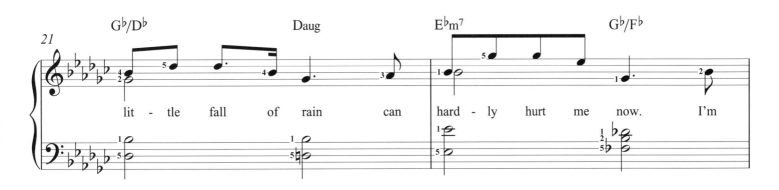

lit - tle fall of rain can hard - ly hurt me now. I'm

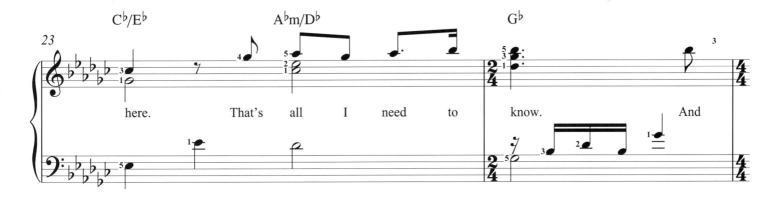

here. That's all I need to know. And

you will keep me safe. And you will keep me close. And

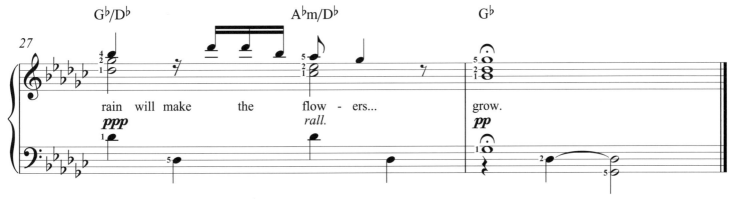

rain will make the flow - ers... grow.

5

A Heart Full Of Love

Music by Claude-Michel Schönberg
Original Lyrics by Alain Boublil & Jean-Marc Natel
English Lyrics by Herbert Kretzmer

At The End Of The Day

Music by Claude-Michel Schönberg
Original Lyrics by Alain Boublil & Jean-Marc Natel
English Lyrics by Herbert Kretzmer

day stand - ing a - bout, what is it for?
win - ter is com - ing on fast, read - y to kill.

1.
One day less to be liv - ing?
One day near - er to

2.
dy - ing.

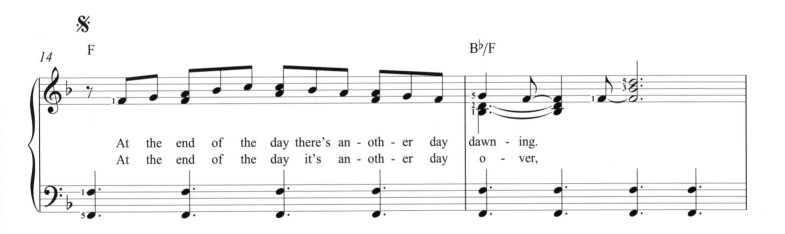

At the end of the day there's an - oth - er day dawn - ing.
At the end of the day it's an - oth - er day o - ver,

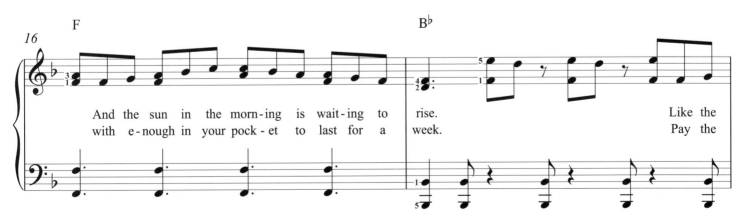

And the sun in the morn - ing is wait - ing to rise. Like the
with e - nough in your pock - et to last for a week. Pay the

Castle On A Cloud

Music by Claude-Michel Schönberg
Original Lyrics by Alain Boublil & Jean-Marc Natel
English Lyrics by Herbert Kretzmer

Bring Him Home

Music by Claude-Michel Schönberg
Lyrics by Alain Boublil & Herbert Kretzmer

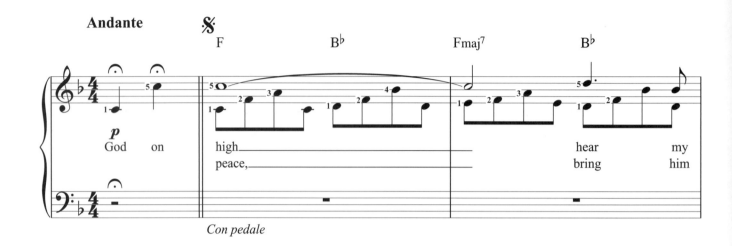

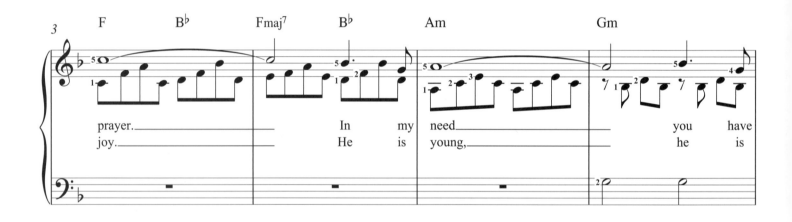

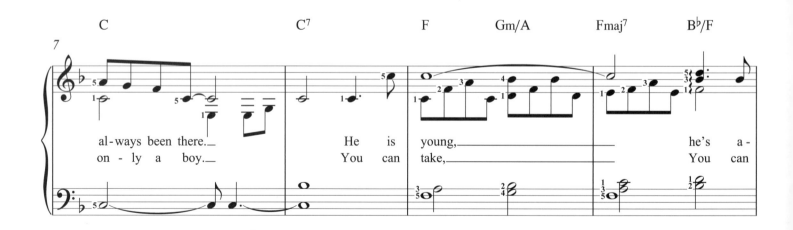

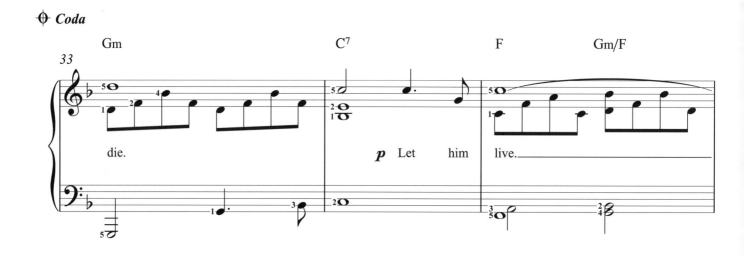

Do You Hear The People Sing?

Music by Claude-Michel Schönberg
Original Lyrics by Alain Boublil & Jean-Marc Natel
English Lyrics by Herbert Kretzmer

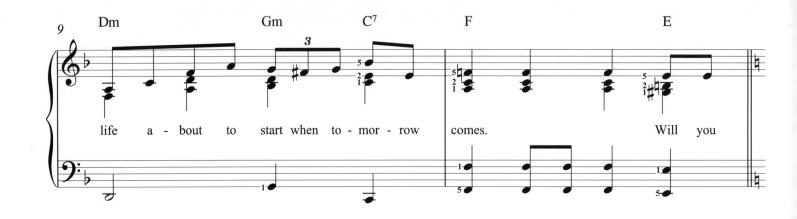

life a-bout to start when to-mor-row comes. Will you

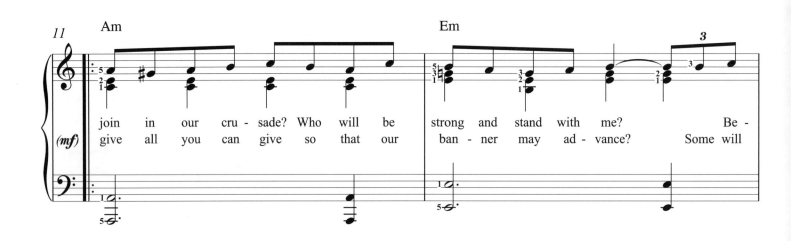

join in our cru-sade? Who will be strong and stand with me? Be-
give all you can give so that our ban-ner may ad-vance? Some will

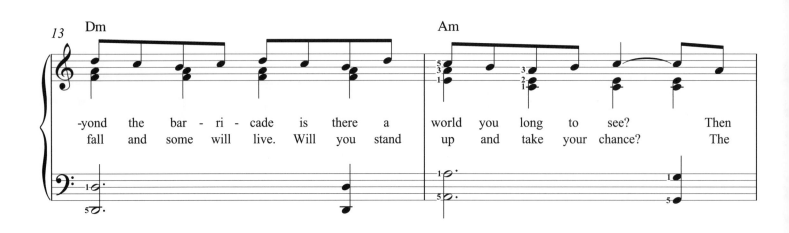

-yond the bar-ri-cade is there a world you long to see? Then
fall and some will live. Will you stand up and take your chance? The

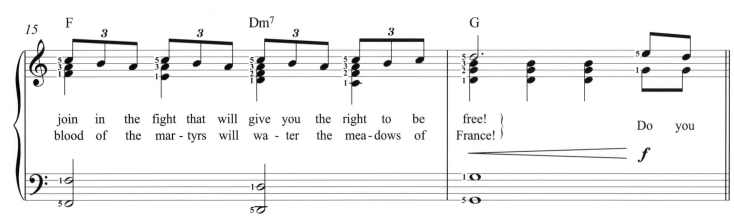

join in the fight that will give you the right to be free! Do you
blood of the mar-tyrs will wa-ter the mea-dows of France!

Drink With Me (To Days Gone By)

Music by Claude-Michel Schönberg
Lyrics by Alain Boublil & Herbert Kretzmer

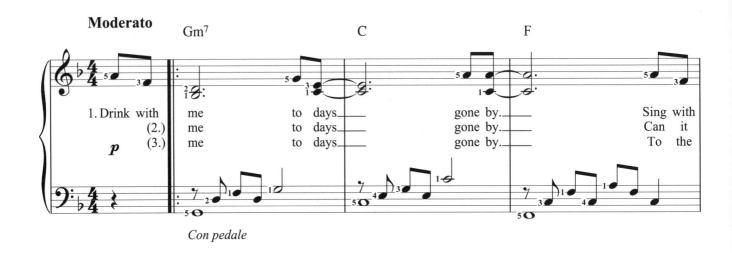

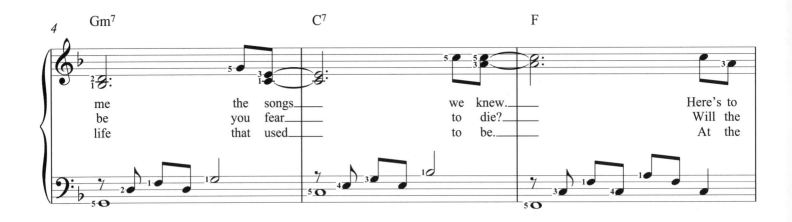

1.

F   Gm⁷   C

went   to   our   beds.   Here's to   them   and   here's   to
noth - ing   at   all?   Is   your
nev - er   run   dry.   Here's to

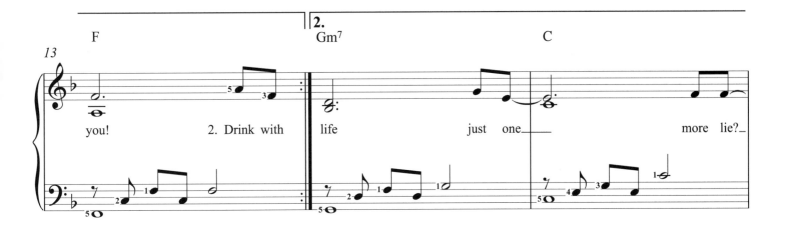

2.

F   Gm⁷   C

you!   2. Drink with   life   just   one____   more   lie?__

3.

F   Gm⁷   C   F

____   3. Drink with   you   and here's____   to   me.____   Here's to

rit.

Gm⁷   C⁷   F

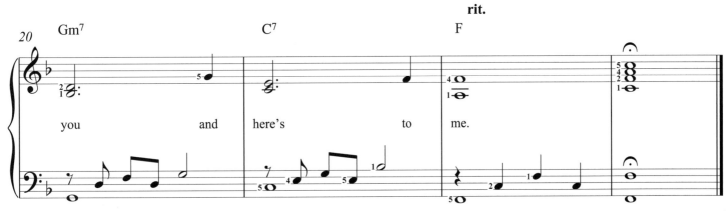

you   and   here's   to   me.

Empty Chairs At Empty Tables

Music by Claude-Michel Schönberg
Lyrics by Alain Boublil & Herbert Kretzmer

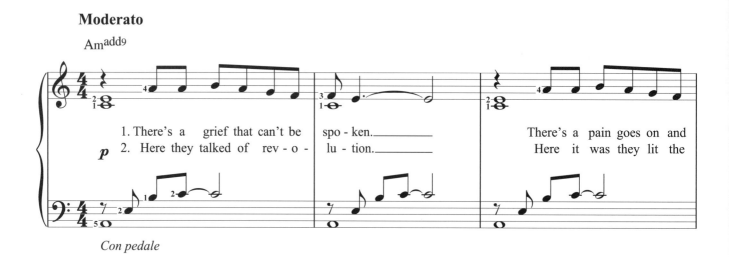

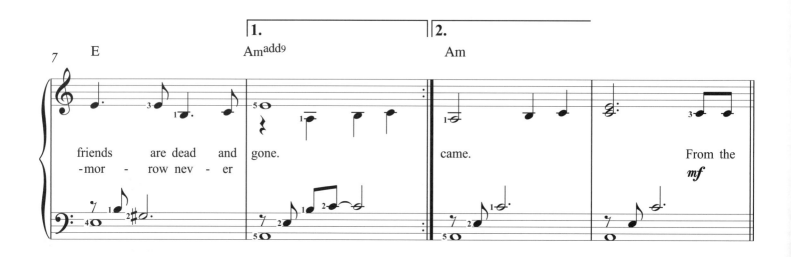

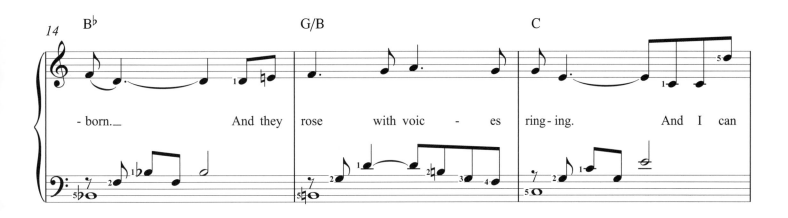

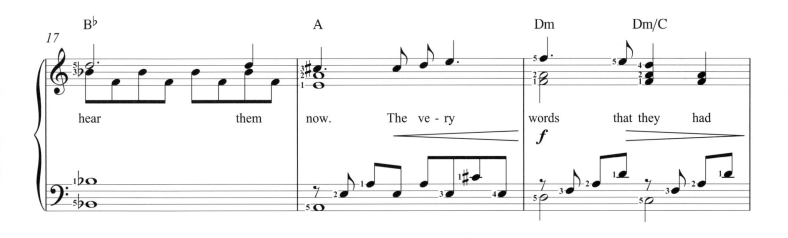

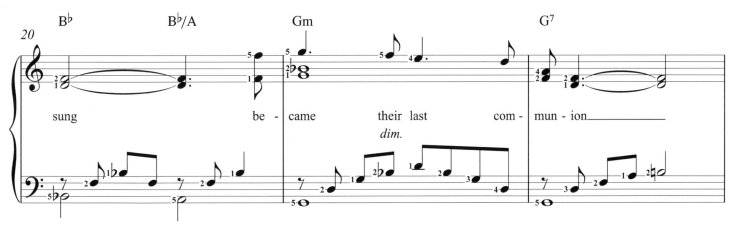

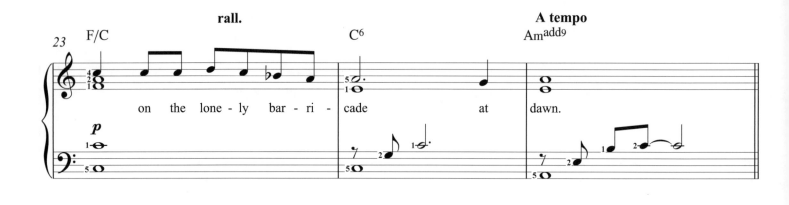

on the lone - ly bar - ri - cade at dawn.

Oh my friends, my friends, for - give me_____

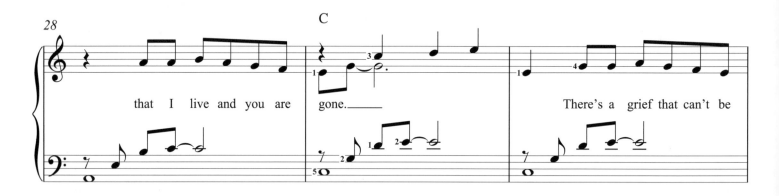

that I live and you are gone._____ There's a grief that can't be

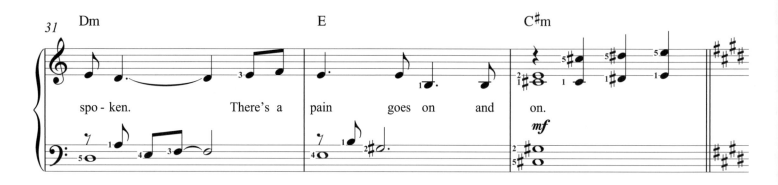

spo - ken. There's a pain goes on and on.

Phan - tom fac - es at the win - dow,_____ phan - tom sha - dows on the

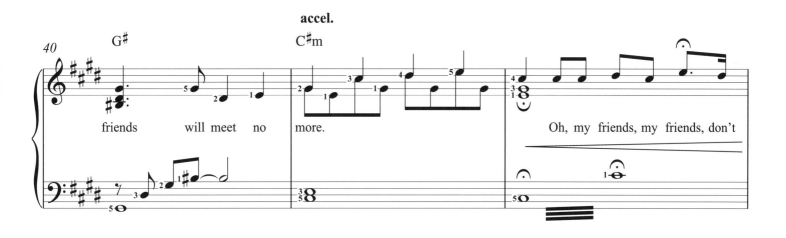

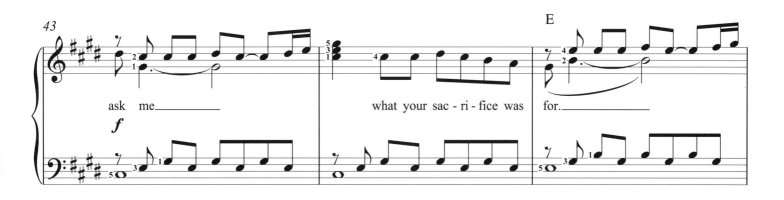

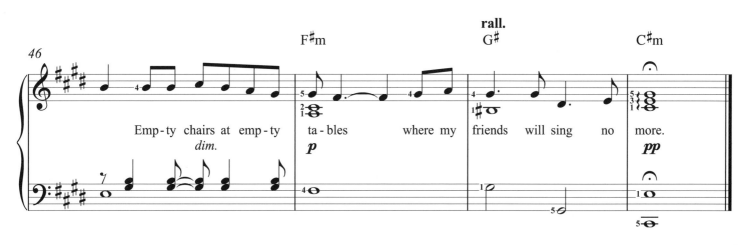

I Dreamed A Dream

Music by Claude-Michel Schönberg
Original Lyrics by Alain Boublil & Jean-Marc Natel
English Lyrics by Herbert Kretzmer

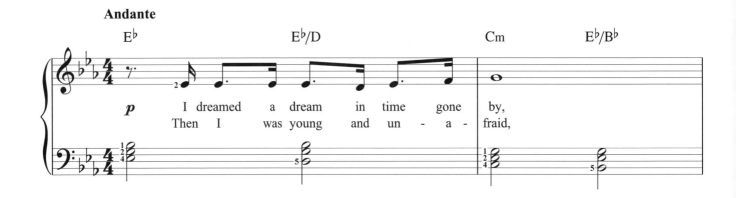

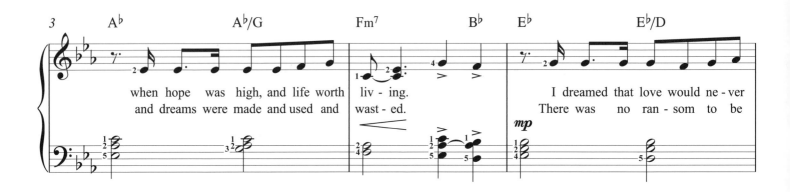

On My Own

Music by Claude-Michel Schönberg
Original Lyrics by Alain Boublil & Jean-Marc Natel
English Lyrics by Herbert Kretzmer, Trevor Nunn & John Caird

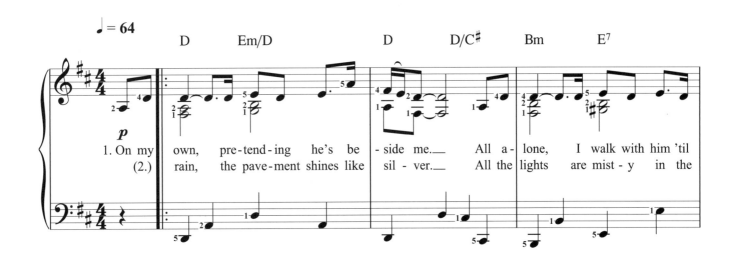

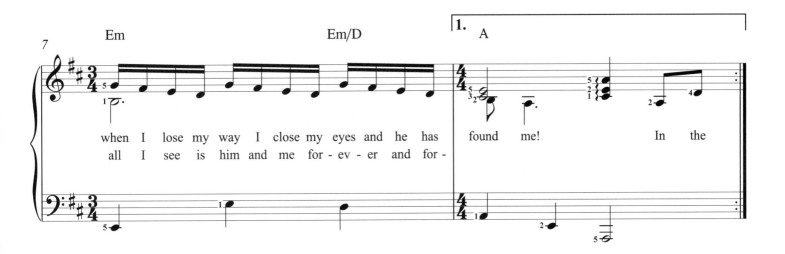

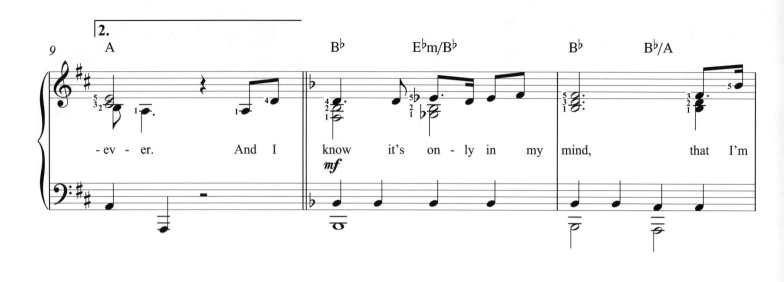

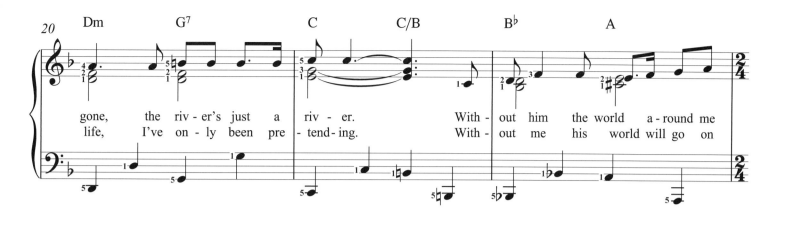

gone, the riv-er's just a riv-er. With - out him the world a - round me
life, I've on-ly been pre - tend-ing. With - out me his world will go on

chang-es. The trees are bare and ev'ry-where the streets are full of stran-gers. 2. I
turn-ing. A world that's full of hap-pi-ness that I have nev-er

1.

2.

known. I love him, _____ I love him, _____ I

rit.

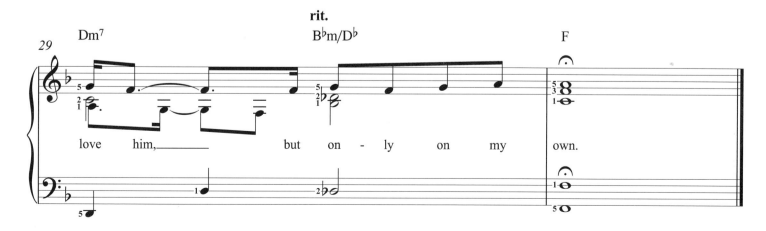

love him, _____ but on - ly on my own.

Look Down (Gavroche)

Music by Claude-Michel Schönberg
Original Lyrics by Alain Boublil & Jean-Marc Natel
English Lyrics by Herbert Kretzmer

Master Of The House

Music by Claude-Michel Schönberg
Original Lyrics by Alain Boublil & Jean-Marc Natel
English Lyrics by Herbert Kretzmer

Tells a sauc-y tale, makes a lit-tle stir, cus-tom-ers ap-pre-ci-ate a

bon vi - veur. Glad to do a friend a fa - vour.

Does-n't cost me to be nice. But noth-ing gets you noth-ing, ev-

- 'ry-thing has got a lit-tle price.

Mas-ter of the house. Keep-er of the zoo,

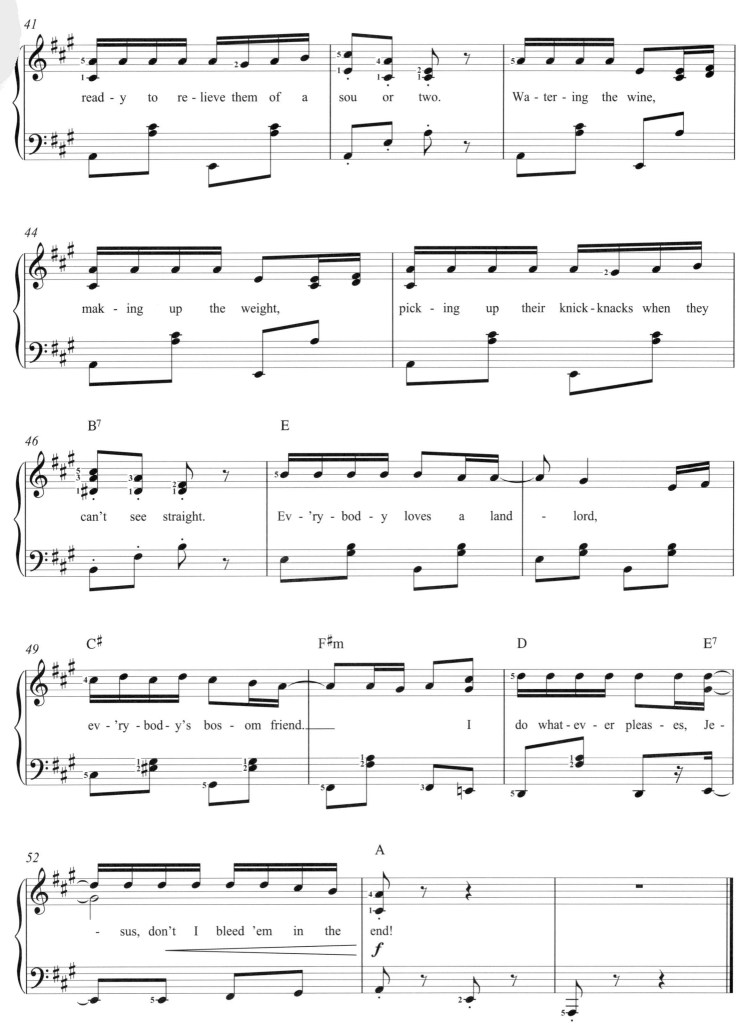

Stars

Music by Claude-Michel Schönberg
Lyrics by Alain Boublil & Herbert Kretzmer

Suddenly

Music by Claude-Michel Schönberg
Lyrics by Herbert Kretzmer and Alain Boublil

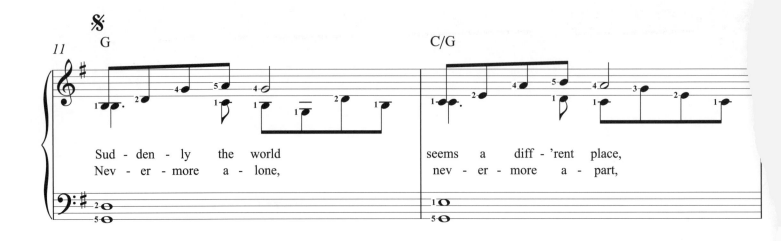

Sud - den - ly the world / Nev - er - more a - lone,

seems a diff - 'rent place, / nev - er - more a - part,

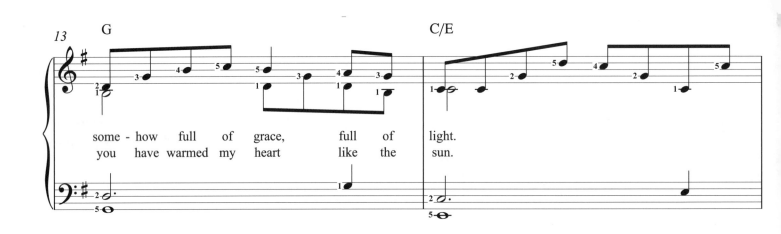

some - how full of grace, / you have warmed my heart

full of / like the

light. / sun.

rit.

How was I to know that so much / You have brought the gift of life and

hope was held in - side me? / love so long de - nied me.

A tempo

To Coda

What is past is gone. / Sud - den - ly I see

Now we jour - ney on through the night.

44

Who Am I?

Music by Claude-Michel Schönberg
Original Lyrics by Alain Boublil & Jean-Marc Natel
English Lyrics by Herbert Kretzmer

Who am I? Can I con-demn this man to slav-e-ry, pre-tend I do not see his

a - go- ny? This in-no-cent who wears my face who goes to judge-ment in my place, who am

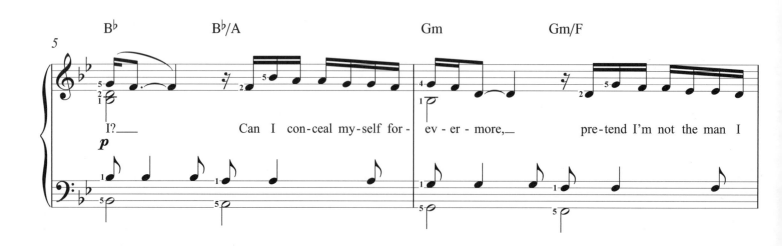

I?___ Can I con-ceal my-self for- ev- er- more,___ pre-tend I'm not the man I